Your order is now equipped for shipping

poems by

Mark Young

Sandy Press

California

Your order is now equipped for shipping, by Mark Young

ISBN: 978-1-7368160-5-9

Cover preparation
by harry k stammer

Cover image
Birchip
by Mark Young

Printed in U.S.A.

Sandy Press
California
https://sandy-press.com/

sandypress@gmail.com

cont'd

A Introduction to *Your order is now equipped for shipping*

By Michael Gottlieb

The poet is talking to himself and as he does, he talks to us. And we need to listen. Not unlike Frank O'Hara walking the streets — but now we're talking about Australia, not Manhattan — at lunchtime, tapping out poems on that Olivetti in Rockefeller Center, this poet walks, drives down dirt roads and paces the 'tiled foyers' of his imagination.

Poems about lost poets — trying to reunite them with their owners. Poems about briefcases — and opening them to find tuna sandwiches. Historical characters make their appearance too: Heidegger, Plato, Dylan (he's 'historical,' right?), The Grimms, Miss Kitty. Poems about Trump and Covid, yes, but also poems about us, all of us, how we live our lives, trying to make sense of all of this. Mark Young shows us how to try. From 'Bricolage:'

> We add
> some
> element; &
>
> what we
> put together
> from what-
> ever is
>
> conveniently
> at hand
>
> lingers, some-
> times
> lasts.

Following on from his *The Codicils, Pelican Dreaming, Genji Monogatari, Songs to Come for the Salamander, Sorties,* and many

5

other books, Mark Young continues to share the poems he writes every day, nearly every day. And we are the better for it. These are poems about what he sees. What he wants to see. What — he knows — we, the readers, need to see. And now we do see.

The last contrail mounts the stairs at midnight.

And we mount those stairs with him.

6.30.22

This Time The Heart Is Electronic Music

I lie on my side on the examination
couch, left arm stretched upwards,
a mirror image of the Statue of Liberty
but without her drapes & torch. Instead
I am covered with electrodes, attached
to various portions of my upper torso.
By straining my neck slightly I can
watch the monitor; &, as the nurse
moves the greased roller ball across
my chest, I see the valves of my heart
opening & closing, opening & closing,
like kissing fish. Then the ECG kicks
in. It becomes a multimedia show,
sound waves displayed across the
bottom of the screen like subtitles to a
foreign movie & a solid bass line that
tells me I am well enough to dance to it.

For four days now

> *Oh, the ragman draws circles*
> *up & down the block*

the unbidden early a.m. song has been one of Dylan's songs from
the mid-sixties,

> *Well, Shakespeare, he's in the alley*
> *with his pointed toes & bells*

a different verse each morning. I don't mind. This is the Dylan

> *Mona tried to tell me*
> *to stay away from the train line*

that I like, the wordsmith *sans pareil*, the fancy dancer, the
Bojangles of the bards. The obligations met, the anthems
finished; & now, in his "Blonde on Blonde" days, he's having fun.

> *Grandpa died last week*
> *& now he's buried in the rocks*

It's the Dylan I keep coming back to. &, since so far we're only
four verses in, it seems that for the next week or so I'll continue

> *To be stuck inside of Mobile*
> *with the Memphis Blues again.*

Revival Meeting

The scattering phase
shifts, then changes in

the electron's canonical
momentum—even for

Heidegger authentic death
with its funky retro feel &

bold designs was a reprieve
from the pre-schismatic

Orthodox worship of the
ancient Christian West.

Papal Bull

Turned off the
highway, only
to find 28 kilo-
meters of dirt
road ahead of
him. Pulled to
the side to think
about what to
do. Recalled
what the late
Pope did on
arrival in a new
country. So,
got out of the
car, bent down
to the road,
& sealed it
with a kiss.

Jean, dansant

It was a temp-
oral regression
from which
he returned

singing *La
Marseillaise*
between mouth-
fuls of an egg &

lettuce sand-
wich. Arch-
ival footage
shows there

were times
when he had
all four feet
off the ground.

life/style changes

tomorrow
i begin my
studies to
become a
transplant

surgeon
the day
after that
i take my
finals exam

it's a series
of multiple
choice
questions—
much easier

for the
tutors to
mark—
along the
lines of

"on what
basis do you
select the
set of scrubs
to wear?"

□ the color of your eyes
□ what makes your ass smaller
□ value for price
□ what most displays your shapely legs
□ what best shows off your tats

tick the box
all questions
are similar
all answers
are correct

one day for
the scores
to be collated
another for the
marks to be

disseminated
a day set aside
for celebration
maybe a day to
practice by my-

self but in a
week i begin my
new career as a
brain transplant
specialist

Travel

broadens the
mind they tell
me; but as with
so many things
the words — 'mind'
& 'travel' — have
to be carefully
defined before the
statement has
veracity. Other-
wise I'd consider
it a false premise
since I've just
traveled to the local
supermarket from
where, induced by
a plethora of rude
& inconsiderate be-
havior, I have re-
turned a narrow-
minded asshole.

Bass line

Most of the
time I'm a
Bb kind of
guy, light
blues, laid-
back, drifting
along with
only the
occasional
backbeat
snare rap
or Mingusian
bass run
added for
emphasis. No-
body knows—
& even I
forget some-
times—that
there's a
Toccata &
Fugue in D
Minor tux
hanging in
the ward-
robe eager
to emerge
with all the
stops out.

The Friendly Witness

Last month, at the
Harmony Palace
restaurant, banquet

politics was ditched
in favor of com-
promise. With history

constantly zigzagging
around, the single
track has become a

bottleneck, & linear
teleology dropped
in favor of a tribal

circling which appears
to completely contradict
our ideas of a usable

piece of furniture. I am
broke as hell. I take
the witness stand for

a second day. Someone
is manipulating me
using mind magic.

Meanwhile, in the Himalayas

In his first public
statement since taking
an unknown dose of
organophosphate insecticide
the King of Nepal
said that he was

struck speechless by
the notation, fingering &
keyboard diagrams under-
lying the stylistic aspects
of the artwork of
Wassily Kandinsky. How

by the removal of one
element of cDNA they
could be used as
sex-pheromone traps
to lure bloodsucking
insects to their deaths.

re/posit

Hope
fully

hope won't
fade, even when
thoughts & patience
both grow thin. Faith
fully persisting, hoping
to collide with luck, to
find rubies in the rain-
forest, a gryphon
in the garden, a
poem in the center
of the crash site.

½-assed

Half-started poems
clutter my briefcase.
Building up but never
built upon. The reverse
of taking your lunch
to work & leaving it
untouched. In there also

other things. Meeting
notes. Presentations. Got
up today to talk about
open repositories. Took
out the wrong bundle.
Half a poem. Tuna &
salad. No mayonnaise.

There are or will be

No Polar Bears in his hometown of Appleton, Wisconsin.
No Polar Bears in your hat.
No Polar Bears in aggregations.
No Polar Bears in the Qatari Desert.
No Polar Bears in Antarctica.
No Polar Bears in bikinis on the side of the road holding signs.
No Polar Bears in cars.
No Polar Bears in Arizona so no posts tagged © Tumblr, Inc.
No Polar Bears in the home market.
No Polar Bears in Coca-Cola's Super Bowl Campaign but a role
for the audience.
No Polar Bears in Scandanavia.
No Polar Bears in Hornstrandir.
No Polar Bears in Poland.
No Polar Bears in a Reliant.
No Polar Bears in South Africa.
No Polar Bears in Mexico.
No Polar Bears in Costa Rica.
No Polar Bears in the provincial park.
No Polar Bears in mission control.
No Polar Bears in the land of flightless birds.
No Polar Bears in a molecule—or is that Polar Bonds?
No Polar Bears in the aforementioned book.
No Polar Bears in Alaska. This is in error.
No Polar Bears in the area.
No Polar Bears in our streets.
No Polar Bears in penguin huddles.
No Polar Bears in the way.
No Polar Bears in the wild.
No Polar Bears in 20 years.
No Polar Bears in 10 Years.
No Polar Bears in the zoo.
No Polar Bears in sight.

No Polar Bears.

I could only hope

Recently I found a poet running around in a grocery store parking lot, & I went through the steps of trying to find her owner. This has not been the first time I've tried to reunite a lost poet with their owner so it got me thinking. I see posts on Facebook all the time of people who've found a poet & don't know what to do, so I figured I would throw this instructable together, & hopefully it will help reunite more lost poets with their owners.

Step 1: Approach with Caution

If you see a lost poet on the street & you are good enough to want to help them, approach with caution. Not all poets are friendly, & not all are vaccinated. Make sure you read the body language of the poet & make sure you approach slowly. Always let the poet sniff your hand before trying to touch them.

If the poet is injured, take them to the nearest vet immediately.

Step 2: Check for Tags

Once you have the lost poet, check the tags. Hopefully the owner has tags on the poet, & those tags have survived whatever the poet has gone through since being lost.

Step 3: Check for a microchip

If the poet doesn't have tags, the next thing you can check for is a microchip.

Step 4: Post that you found this poet everywhere!

If the poet doesn't have tags or a microchip the next best chance you have of finding the owner is spreading the word.

When people are looking for their lost poets they will check a variety of places.

Craigslist

If you post on craigslist, be very careful. If anyone asks you for money it's probably a scam. Always ask for proof of ownership. If this is truly the owner, they will have some sort of proof including pictures, vet records, or paperwork from when they adopted/bought the poet.

Facebook

If you have a facebook account, post that you found a poet & ask your friends to share. When I posted it got shared 300 times! Post on pages or groups that are designed for lost & found poets. For example "Lost & Found Poets Washington State." Again, if someone contacts you, ask for proof of ownership & be wary of anyone who asks for money.

Local shelter (Humane Society, ASPCA, etc)

Often times if someone has lost their poet they will contact the local shelter. They generally have databases of lost & found poets.

Local Veterinarians

If the person who lost their poet is local it's likely that their vet is local as well. You can call the vet with a description of the poet & they may recognize it.

If you still don't hear from the owner it's time to take the next step.

Step 5: Take the poet to a local shelter

Do some research & find a no-kill shelter.

The shelter will have some sort of protocol. At the shelter where I took the poet I found they hold it for 10 days for the owner to come forward, & then put it up for adoption.

Hopefully the owner will come forward, & if not, hopefully the poet will be adopted. Take comfort in knowing you did everything you could.

The Poem About The Poem

came so easily I could not wait
to start / the poem. & yet,
ironically, it was this eagerness
to get on with it that made the
starting difficult. I thought I knew
the journey, knew how the
poem would shape & show
itself. Instead found almost nothing,
a few pieces of past so brittle
that they crumbled as the mind
alighted on them. & in this absence
of obvious landmarks realized
that most of our life is not
momentous, is instead made up
of a series of minor moments that dart
back & forth between each other,
underpinning & overlaying, being
added to until each series achieves
a momentum of its own, a thread
worn smooth by time where I,
impatient, had hoped to find a
knotted cord, a message stick.

Ryongchŏn — for the xenophobic amnesiacs

So large an explosion
that only from space

can it be seen entire.
So long a policy of

isolation that it takes
a day to recall there

is a world outside
& call on it for help.

Dear John McCain

Watching you
on the first of the
debates, can I
just say that
the more you
try to distance
yourself from
George W. Bush
the more you
end up sounding
just like him. &
from where I'm
sitting on the
other side of
the ocean, eight
years of lies &
ineptitude is
already eight
years too many.

Even though

the jokes
weren't all
that funny

everybody
laughed

because
it was The
President

telling them.

Same old
same old

but with a
significant
difference.

This time
they were
laughing
with him,

not at him
like they
did with

the fuckwit
who was the
previous

POTUS.

For Veterans' Day

Donald J. Trump had
a sweatshop in Myanmar
run him up a Buddha
the size of the ones that
used to be at Bamiyan

with a hand at the end
of an elevator arm in
which he was carried
up from the stage to a
height approximately

equal to 2000 bodies
stacked one on top of
another & from where
he delivered a speech
that was amplified /

televised / digitalized /
YouTubized so that the
whole world could
know what the sound of
one hand crapping was.

Daybreaker

Effervescence—is that
how you spell it? I
download the same
Java update over &
over in the hope
that it will slip one time
& bring me a cup of
genuine Kenya Mocha
but it won't because
geography was never
my best subject. All
I get are offers of
discount bulk buys on
Tibetan prayer wheels
& dvds of Appalachian
revivalist meetings with
a complimentary snake
thrown in. I respond to
all the scam spam
asking me to update my
account at banks I've
never used, give my
name as Trump, 1100
S. Ocean Blvd, Fl 34880.

Life & Death as Gus Hoo sees it

All of a sudden, the game
changed. & I had to close
it down. I closed down the
greatest economy ever in
history. & then, I closed it
down. & now we're opening

it. & we saved, by the way,
by closing it, we saved mill-
ions of lives. If we would
have gone to herd, & we
knew very little about the
disease, if we would have

gone herd, we would have
lost millions of people. Mill-
ions of people. One person's
too much. We're at 140,000
people. One person is too
much. We're at 140,000. We

would have lost millions of
people. & those people that
really understand it, really
understand it, they said it's
incredible, the job that we've

done.

Almost one year on

I go looking for
the speeches of
Donald J. Trump
but all I can find
are comic cut-ups.

I go looking for
any memorable
quotes but all I
can find are
those purloined
from Roy Cohn.

I go looking for
images of him loo-
king presidential
but all I can find
are moments of
absolute cupidity.

these news pics persist

Elsewhere there is video
footage of the stretcher
bearers pausing so the
Secretary of Homeland

Security can draw back
the covers & identify
which parts of the visual
culture in the San Fran-

cisco Bay Area still have
some life in them & might,
therefore, constitute a
homegrown terrorist threat.

Corporate greed

adheres to the
principle that
pigmentation genes
& ancestry are
there to be ex-
ploited, & the
pursuit of money
is a spiritual task.

Karaoke

Even before the sales
meeting was properly
underway the
merchandizer for
the North-West was re-
stocking the shelves.
"This talk of synergy
is making me hungry. The
Mona Lisa combined
calendar & teatowel might
be the most popular line
in the cities, but out
where I come from
it's still very much
vacuum tubes & butter
churns. Ten-page previews
& ten-second spots by
once-famous talking
heads just don't cut it
when things grow
wild. It's tomato season—
primary colors hang
from the vines. What
more could they want?"

Bricolage

We add
some
element; &

what we
put together
from what-
ever is

conveniently
at hand

lingers, some-
times
lasts.

Cursive script

I sit
in a chair
in a room lit
only by the
lost light
of late
evening

eating
dried fruit
from a mini-
pack made
of a dull
paper that
stamps its own
taste upon the
contents

& think about
moving
to a house in
the country
where the words
don't have to
be summoned

but come
of their own
accord when
they're ready
to be
milked.

Letter to a young poet

Setting out to visit all
those wonderful places
that your mother sends

postcards from is no ex-
cuse for not working —
remember that travel

is often confused with
travail. & be aware that
pterodactyls will come at

you with the sun at their
backs, *tout comme ta maman,*
whom they closely resemble.

Meanwhile

So many things
beginning with the
same letter. No
wonder he was
confused. The court-
yard empty & the
flowers turned
into dust. Never-
theless he pressed
on with it. Small
animals were
drawn to him.

Ganeesh is living in a duplex down the road

Every so often
he would pause
in the pursuit of
wildebeeste, all-

owing the child
within to inhale
the breath of
centaurs. Then

he would come
up for air or
violence or what-
ever the current

coin of the realm
is around here.

Do / the loco / motion with me

Isaac Newton is in the room. I wake to the strains of "For every action…" being recited. The red light of the powerboard is on & unblinking. I can sense no physical presence; I think it is the powerboard that is channeling Newton. The why I have no idea.

"There is an equal & opposite reaction." I have a sudden vision of the Swedish border. A metal bar across a transit point which is raised when somebody wishes to enter or to leave the country. But "equal & opposite." So therefore it means that only if someone leaves can someone else enter.

I'm not too sure if it is actually Sweden. It seems to me my vision has more to do with the kingdoms of the *Game of Thrones*. I retreat to Newton's first law: "Every object moves in a straight line unless acted upon by a force." My knowledge base is the object, my imagination is the force that acts upon it, to move it slightly off-course.

All very transitory, however. I turn the lamp on which interrupts the Newtonian flow. Something to do with shear rate; though the sheer rate of equations is way beyond both my knowledge base & my imagination. Ancient Westeros, modern Sweden, both vanish, replaced by the sorts of things one finds on a bedside table — air-con remote, eye drops, tissues, moisturizer, books.

I turn the lamp off. Light continues to flow. & now it's Einstein who's in the room. I pull the pillow over my head. The light is minimized but the words get through. "The speed of light in a vacuum is constant."

Code-X

Material is as Madonna does. The
fine print smells otherwise; though

seems to read the same, even if it
is in braille. Cryptography's for

other people he would often say.
He'd lost interest in it, ever since the

time he'd had trouble swallowing a
Rubik's cube. It didn't translate either.

A Paumanok Picture

Later, when the road
had opened,
Walt Whitman
was allowed to pass.

maybe this will help you

The dream about snow monkeys
is one of the less common
dreams. Not absolutely unique,

but rare enough. Time to take
your ukelele out of long-term
storage & sing along. Here is

the chord structure, here are
some diagrams showing where
your fingers should be placed.

chiaroscuro

Light is de-
ception, is
shape shifter,
given to giving
        shadow
    to things that
have no substance
    in the dark.

Tourmaline

&

eigenvalues

& the
other

faint

shifts & drifts

that
transcribe
the
window

in
place

of
rain.

My orchid is dying

Leave the spike intact. You'll
hear a hissing sound & see
air bubbles rise. The windward
pile driver may damage the
stems & leaves of nearby
buildings but will probably

leave the *teppanyaki* bar
unscathed. Don't wear white
unless you're either part of the
entertainment, or a well-equipped
games room with a bowling
alley & countless televisions.

Jocasta Quits In Protest

Facing political persecution, &
concerned that a war of words
on the subject of replacement hor-
mone therapy was being waged
against her by Augustine, the

Bishop of Hippo, via a series of mis-
spelled tweets, she signaled to the
camera operator to cut away from
her & focus on the small window set
high up in the otherwise blank back

wall. Then, in a voice-over, she calmly
said: "When the Bishop asks — & he
will — what is the highest meaning of
the sacred truth, just answer *vast
emptiness, nothing holy* & walk away."

Why species decline

Some scientists believe
that the broad-beaked
asparagus has a gambling
addiction. That is why it
chooses to live a solitary
existence on an equally
solitary rocky island some-
where in the lower reaches

of the Atlantic Ocean. Now
it only ventures to the casinos
of Macau once the regular
mating season is over, when the
chances of finding a mate
have become extremely low.

viva voce

> She picks up a word, in-
> spects it. The scratches
> on its surface imply
> it's been used too many
> times already. Same with
> the next one she picks up.
> A new lexicon beckons.

Structural Humiliation

> Pop culture historians take
> their art seriously but see
> little else. Houses can be
>
> eaten by termites & fall,
> multinational corporations
> reap profits by taking out
>
> patents on indigenous plants,
> the Civil War turn into an
> antique furniture business,
>
> & all they can say is "OMG!
> The shoes are outdated & the
> sock colors are inaccurate."

The foundation for the renovations

In the city of Alma they came a-
cross with an export development
plan saying why they love to
show their horses. You should
not have to write more than that,
not have to explicitly define a

purpose. Somewhere Derrida
pointed out that deconstruction
represents a spirit of tireless
critical vigilance against all claims
to final possession of the truth of
absolute justice. But the city is a

melting pot, can be enormously
stressful, like houses glimpsed
through fog along narrow streets.
Make your voice heard & help
fight the assault. How far has the
apple fallen from Plato's tree?

Glockenspiel

The *meistersingers* of Düsseldorf
roam the streets, ostensibly to

recite poems but in reality
looking for ways to make more

money off of passers-by by re-
fining their ability to extrapolate

data from clothing & shoe sizes,
then using it to find what skeletons

are buried where & which seem
most favorable for blackmail.

Eventually

Acrobats abound on the benches
of the transit lounge. Everyone
else is staying clear, washing their
hands in rosewater or anointing
their brows with the blood of
pygmy possums. Curtains are
drawn across the picture wind-
ows, dampening down the noise

of luggage trolleys, keeping out
the sun. It may be we are all
waiting for flights out; but since
there are no flights scheduled out
into the future, this may be where
we have decided to make a stand.

A gracious residential area

A tiled foyer leads into a
golf course perched above
the Mediterranean. Lipstick
pink might not be the right
choice for working at a start-
up, but we clearly don't know
how to make any better life
choices, especially when
someone has just teed off &
the ball is heading down the
hallway in our direction. Will
the dealer take the car back?
How long does mediation
usually take? What's that say-
ing about a piece of string?

For Max Ernst

The elephant of the Celebes dances
mainly at night. The sun is too
bright for her, blurs the rhythm so
the nuances are lost. But even then
she is guided by the drumming of
her feet.

An accolyte of de Chirico
points the elephant of the Celebes
towards the *corrida*. There she is
introduced as The Sumatran Pachy-
derm but given no *estoque* since she
has nowhere to carry it. Besides,
she has her own tusks.

On May Day
Gay Day the elephant of the Celebes
has sufficient leather to cover those
in the Parade that fancy it. She com-
promises, wears a shiny metal cuff.
Brightly-colored acolytes crowd her
conning tower, create a contrast to
her battleship gray. The entire brings
both penises of the bystander erect.

Kingfisher assimilation

Charles Olson sits on the
fence near the letter-box,
turquoise frockcoat out-
standing in the early sun-
light. His waistcoat seems
washed out in comparison,
almost stained, but it has
a subtlety of color about it

that one gradually becomes
attuned to. He has changed
somewhat since the last time
I set eyes on him, has become
his own avatar. What has not
changed is the will to change.

Random enthalpy or random entropy?

The last contrail mounts the
stairs at midnight. Music
surrounds it; *Finlandia* by
Sibelius; which may be why
the ascent is so quiet, even
though the music does not
penetrate the contrail's
senses. The typewriter it

carries with it has passed
the becoming a burden
stage. Should have been left
behind some time back; but a
contract is a contract, & even
though Bashō has long passed,
there's still that clause in there,
passes to his heirs & successors.

awestruck / by a / super blood moon

The signal strength of
the patient's perception
of his inner self sucks. That's

a clinical expression—take it
to mean that his concept
"false-self" is probably

not aligned with the
vertical centerline of
the business communities

of Southern California
but with the distal end of a
dog. If not that then it's

because he wears high heels
& tries to save a few bucks
here & there on his power bill.

La Golondrina

The last Abencerrages king of Granada
sought neither pleasant fruit nor
limpid fountains. Rather it was a
Greater Set of Questions-&-Answers
as to why setting is extremely important

to *The Great Gatsby*. A similar measure
began on the southern border with Mexico
where conspiracy theories can spread
as fast as a virus & where fireworks-
related deaths & injuries are on the rise.

Now it's moved beyond the place where
it began, typically between 150 & 175
decibels when accompanied by piano,
ukulele, or accordion. Not just fireworks
that can be hazardous to your health.

A breakthrough study

She used her Cisna commune eve-
ry now & then. Category: place
without polygons. There's a huge

range up north this time of year.
Her idea of fertility was to be ex-
pected. A practical past running

from actual or perceived danger —
possibly a predator — was conjured
up by sporting show-biz types who

were as counterfeit as she was, &
who prescribed a round of mediation
that utilizes a $2 million system

which provides multilingual staff
in addition to positive expectations.

(s)light

I think back on what she
said. There is distortion,
Chinese whispers, so that
I can't decipher if it was

*always stay downwind of
interlopers* or *always wind
down after riding an ant-
elope* was what she meant.

Doesn't matter. Either
sounds fine in a poem,
& to be able to use them
both together is a bonus.

The will

This mechanism, with
few unique items, no
longer displayed. A
rectangle duplicates
its movements, but
uses makeshift words.

Is it strange that
an existing evil on
which diplomacy
stands turns a much
greater profit than
causal incarnation?

Such humor is not ex-
pected. He circumvents
it, but doesn't quite
know how to promote
himself. How dare this
object know what to do?

Her thirty-third studio album

Miss Kitty tweets that
the extreme weather
sweeping the world

has left New York City
reeling as it realizes
there are now less

than 50 pre-mixed cock-
tails in their plastic jars
left in the entire city.

forensic tarantellas

The blonde woman spent
her years of pilgrimage
watching security tapes gene-
rated by a patriarchal system
of law enforcement that
lacked ethics & accountability.
Now she runs an interactive
dance workshop. Some of the

movements are taken from
the interrogation of prisoners
she saw there. Others she
found as random words in
Petrarch's sonnets. *Who keeps
following me?* she wonders.

I / tried to / real her back

After a year of witty
banter, the first firemen
at the scene said "start the
conversation with an open-
ended question, otherwise
bumps will appear at the
injection sites." It's really
a form of manipulation,

they agreed, but the only
other thing that might
possibly negate the out-
break is the arrival of a
new flavor of ice cream,
& that's hard to arrange.

A letter to Matsuo Bashō

Each morning, in the later
part of the season, two
rainbow lorikeets arrive &
perch in the upper branches
of the mandarin tree, sitting
there, couple-comfy, until
I have finished my garden
duties. Then they move to
the lower branches to eat the
ripest fruit, piercing the skin
& attacking the flesh. Some
skins & segments fall to the
ground. Other leavings remain,
stalks stuck to the wood, hollow
orange shells, miniatures of
those lanterns you like so much.

Detected in a second regional town.

I don't know if I can ever go back to
the low-rise jean trend now that no
part of Earth's surface is immune from
illegal pot growing operations such
as those in the Antelope Valley, even
though it is only accessible by a six
mile causeway. Distance is obviously
no deterrent; & now victims from East
Asia & Sub-Saharan Africa have been
discovered in the waterways. Put it down
to those simplistic policies pursued
actively by governments & which are
now shown to have spatial consequences.
If you want further information, a free
eBook is included when you shop for
the Mini Sac Leather Tote Bag online.

I think there's a thirties musical that goes . . .

Evidence of increasing age includes
painting by numbers with your eyes
closed. That way the fact that you
don't have any art tools is of little
import. The sweep across the backs
of your eyelids is what matters, can
be dramatic when what you've done
is satisfying, or act as a form of wind-
shield wiper that clears away debris,
or poor color choices, or any other
thing that gets in the way. Don't for-
get that the last line is left in limbo.

Slow Juggernaut

The structure. Incline, endocrine. Faint
taste of the roundabouts – various birds,
trees at disparate stages of their fruiting.

The approach is a cautious one. Recline,
exocrine. People patiently wait their
turn. The birds attack the trees. Fruit falls.

The results are disappointing. Supine,
decline. Impatience replaces. Death rates
rise. Empty trees. The birds have flown.

Meanwhile, in the message parlor

The prospectus promises relief from
painful interactions. Doesn't guarantee
it though. Night lights make no sense
during the day. Even if there weren't
tree branches obscuring the walkways
she still couldn't see to read by. It's the
small print that trips you up, every time.

Working on a capsicum farm

Way before television, up & down
the main street on a Saturday night.
Olive oil heated in a large sauce-
pan, a high energy production.
Unanimously well received. Great
feedback for a never say die team.

"The intention is to allow people
to stay living in their own homes,"
Carol explained. "We're hoping
those people who want to become
train drivers will wear white on
the night – lots of lace, no denim.

"It's so rewarding to see them once
they step out of their comfort zone."

A poem ending with a line from *Beowulf*

These videos & wide-
mouth pint size mason
jars introduce you to
the thrill of moving
into a new home when
you don't qualify
for a care package.

I actually heard someone say this:
"From his eyes came a light not fair."

Safe repairs

Repeated exposure to cocaine
is a major cellular substrate
for learning & memory; but in

inexperienced hands the brain
fails to adapt. Without infection
prevention & control guidance

it becomes a premodifying
compound adjective that allows
water ingress through your roof.

Transversing

those walkways for the
visually impaired. Their
proximity, their closing
in. Too much for him, still
not quite comfortable with
varieties of bellicose marsh
hen, or appliqué, or the sur-
feit of tourist buses bound

for pedestrian destinations.
Somewhere near the cusp
he paused to shake out the
senses from his snakeskin
handbag, looking for some-
thing to ease the pain with.

Fifi's Cottage

Again the catafalque party, led
by the 16 Marshmallow Soft Plush
inches of Marcellus The Cactus
Kellytoy, added to the occasion,

mounting the memorial area well
before the installation of park
furniture & trees. Life isn't what
it used to be. Nor, so it seems, is

death, even though the cosy poly-
ester fibers make it machine wash-
able & perfect for younger children
to use as a pillow or nap buddy.

amalgamated every bit of

Because of the cover crop seed &
the fertilizer needed, professional
cyclists in Great Britain have en-
dured nearly 100 years of mediocrity.
Now that new metal has been flown
in for the Miki Miki track, & scattered
fragments of humanity have started
using mercury to recover gold from

the beautiful *cenotes* of Mexico, the
synchronous triggering of multiple
slope failures is a thing of the past.
New bikes can include an onboard
spa & yoga activities; & backlit LCD
screens can show where they've been.

The election will be won on character

Revegetation is underway across a
variety of disciplines in cases where
hospitalization is not required. Re-
gional males now stay at home &
work out dance moves prior to being
critiqued on their choreography.
Elsewhere, following a competitive
procurement process, farmers are

handing in reports of a recent rise
in goat thefts including some found
driving with a relevant drug in their
saliva. Now that tie-dying shirts has
become an Olympic event, only ten
tickets are left for entry to the local fair.

A well-tempered murine sequence

The popular success of Hansel & Gretel was a surprise to the Grimms. In fact, the whole collection of *Kinder- und Hausmärchen* provided a serendipitous way to fund their on-going research into & collecting examples of *Volkspoesie*.

As an aside, they tracked the movement of words across countries & plotted their consonantal drift. How D in one language translates in time to T in another, *und so weiter*. Now known as Grimm's Law, singular, after the elder brother.

A century earlier J. S. Bach had trialled a somewhat similar path in a different field. There is his strange transcription of the *Toccata & Fugue in D Minor* that uses only letters, four of them, C, A, & G, plus D replaced by T. The fugue is base-paired—A is T's counterpoint, G is C's.

The Grimms didn't understand what Bach had been up to, not even the younger who was, supposedly, musically inclined. Beyond them. Beyond everybody for two centuries until 449 scientists & a super-computer finally figured out the mouse genome & went on to publish their results in a multi-authored *Nature* paper.

Letters stand in utter defiance to spelling-book rules

The lost chatter of men, the
exteriority of written &
figurative elements—very
few persons write a good
letter. In this split & drifting

space, strange bonds are knit.
Two garrulous mutes use
elegant language, yet use it
easily. A word can take the
place of an object if the paren-

thesis is avoided. Neatness is
important. The measure of
the "iron horse" is how many
missives it drags behind. No
mass, no name, form without

volume. Word & object are
deployed in two different
dimensions. Emptiness undoes
the space. Verbal lightning
flashes come naturally to a child.

Sources:
This Is Not a Pipe, by Michel Foucault
The Ladies' Book of Etiquette (1860), by Florence Hartley

Enterprises of subversion & destruction

The polished surface throws
back the arrow. Beneath it,
handwritten in a painstaking
artificial script, a script from
the convent, is "an American

may possibly know the customs
of your country better than you
do." Visible form is excavated.
Shape dissipates. About this
ambiguity I am ambiguous.

To reproduce & to articulate; to
imitate & to signify; to look &
to read. What misleads us is the
inevitable futility of converting
the text to some glaring color

when a simple swipe of a rag
could soon erase it & reduce
phoneticism to mere gray noise or
inconspicuous article. Treasure
the pearls of what you have read.

Sources:
This Is Not a Pipe, by Michel Foucault
The Ladies' Book of Etiquette (1860), by Florence Hartley

cantilevered

Can't tell you any-
thing you haven't
heard before. Only
change the timbre /
pitch / accentuate
some different
syllables in the hope
the telling might
come a little closer
to you. It is vanity
                    speaking.

Take Five, Decades Later

Supposedly it is a music
that keeps you young, the
Dave Brubeck Quartet re-
dux, combined age around
300 years, more white hair
than a polar bears'
convention. They try to
belie their age. It is a form
of floating. But. The music.

Is. Old. & without the
transcendent magic of Paul
Desmond they are only
old men going through
the motions / paying the
rent / presenting the past
as it was, not what it should
be with fifty years to change
it in. They want to dance,

but this recycled air is not
for pirouetting. But. They. Go
through some easy steps
until the elderly Brubeck
plays Brahms' *Lullaby* as
an encore for the elderly
audience & everyone & the
elderly band realizes it
is way past their bedtime.

exorcise_exercise

Racquets she said, even though there was no tennis going on.

Or maybe it was *rackets*, & she was talking about the noise up the road, or the way that local builders get their plans through council despite breaching nearly every bylaw in the book.

Could have been *Reckitts*, left up for me to interpret which among their products I'm in dire need of — condoms, antiseptic lotions, mustard, mouthwash, grime or pimple remover.

Then again, perhaps *rickets,* even though I'm not young — except in name — & any or all of the products listed above would have helped minimize or even remove that condition.

So, *rockets.* No, not that, her red glare tells me quite clearly.

Leaves only *ruckets* . . . But there's no such word in general use, though it is a family name, & a brand of skates, &, if Google's autocomplete is accurate, it might have something to do with tickets to the Rugby World Cup.

Though, wait. Because of this fuss I'm making over what the word in question is, I've just been accused of causing a *ruckus.* Perhaps that is what was intended all along.

Dancing on the ceiling

Almost one million
people selling sauerkraut
showed up in
relational data bases

News outlets put
the same sort of spin on it
as they do with the the fact
that acne-prone people
should avoid tuna in case
they react badly to it

Rocks simply weather
into a layer of dust
so thick that a truck
can get stuck in it

Any empirical &/or
hypertextual evaluation
of this information
& the development of

future-proof secondary packaging
for the pharmaceutical industry
shows only that one should
be wary of false promises.

High flow drainage crossings

Umbrellas lined the delay
in work commitments on
her Facebook page. Cited
as a possible reason was the
discovery of four pigs that
had been slaughtered in
bizarre circumstances. Flam-
boyant headpieces will now
be the order of the day says
the Climate Council's *Tonto
thru to the Lone Ranger* report.

Your order is now equipped for shipping

A man runs through London's
Hyde Park. Footage of the im-

mediate aftermath was shared
on social media & now experts

want pork pulled over cancer
concerns. There are important

things to note: summoning
glyphs is completely hereditary

& the Red Sox have no one to
blame for failing but themselves.

**a snapshot of the unbiased views of Sky News
Australia's self-claimed centrist commentators**

Rupert Murdoch denounces 'woke orthodoxy'

Sky News leads the way in claiming that every progressive
cause, from climate action to anti-racism to feminism, signals a
capitulation to woke 'lefty lunacy'

The 'woke agenda' undermines the principles which 'sustained
us for generations'

Ordinary people do not like the politics of woke

'the calling card of the woke left' is to 'attack mainstream
Australians to prove their own superiority'

Woke-left hatred of 'normal' is 'a fear of what it represents' &
'real life is against them'

'Brutal & unforgiving' new 'woke religion' offers no 'absolution'
in sporting world

'Being woke' is an inexcusable defence for just being 'insensitive'
& 'uncivilized'

Schooling overhaul dumbs down kids in push to be 'woke'

so disappointing that we've got another example of this woke
rubbish which is being developed by some of our academics in
our education faculties

'We have evidence that woke politics is making the west
desperately weak'

Australia has become so 'weak' so 'woke' and so 'broke'

China 'relish' in Australia 'rotting' because of woke culture

The woke will 'destroy our language', unless we 'have names for them'

Acknowledgements

Some of these poems have previously appeared in:

A New Ulster, Arteidolia, BlazeVOX, Bones - a journal for the short poem, Datura, Die Leere Mitte, e·ratio, experiential-experimental-literature, Fixator Press, Fleas on the dog, Home Planet News Online, Indefinite Space, Ink Pantry, Lothlorien Poetry Journal, Mad Swirl, Marsh Hawk Review, MisfitMagazine, NAUSEATED DRIVE, Neologism, Offcourse, otata, Poetry WTF?, RIC Journal, Rochford Street Review, Scud, Setu, SurVision, Synapse, Synchronized Chaos, The Sparrow's Trombone, TXTOBJX, Unlikely Stories, Utsanga.it, Yellow Mama, & Ygdrasil.

My thanks to the respective editors.

Two of the poems have also appeared in
a small chapbook, *last words,*
published by Tim Wright's now orries press
in Melbourne, Victoria, Australia.

Bio Note

Photo by Lauren Young

Mark Young was born in Aotearoa New Zealand but now lives in a small town in North Queensland in Australia. He has been publishing poetry for over sixty years, & is the author of around sixty books, primarily text poetry but also including speculative fiction, vispo, non-fiction pieces, & art history.

He is the editor of *Otoliths*.

Other Books by Mark Young from Sandy Press

sorties

The Sasquatch Walks Amonu Us

Songs to Come for the Salamander
Poems 2013 — 2021
Selected and with an introduction
by Thomas Fink
(co-published with Meritage Press)

The above are available through Amazon
or Book Depository.

www.ingramcontent.com/pod-product-compliance
Lightning Source LLC
Chambersburg PA
CBHW060554100426
42742CB00013B/2558